THE
REAGAN
DOCTRINE
AND
BEYOND

D1215795

THE REAGAN DOCTRINE AND BEYOND

Christopher C. DeMuth

Owen Harries

Irving Kristol

Joshua Muravchik

Stephen Rosenfeld

Stephen Solarz

American Enterprise Institute for Public Policy Research
Washington, D.C.

ALBRIGHT COLLEGE LIBRARY

Distributed by arrangement with

UPA, Inc.
4720 Boston Way
Lanham, MD 20706
3 Henrietta Street
London WC2E 8LU, England

Library of Congress Cataloging-in-Publication Data

The Reagan doctrine and beyond / Christopher C. DeMuth
. . . [et al.]. p. cm.
  Speeches delivered at public policy forum, 7/14/87, Amer-
ican Enterprise Institute for Public Policy Research. 1.
United States—Foreign relations—1981–   . 2. Reagan,
Ronald. I. DeMuth, Christopher C. II. American Enterprise
Institute for Public Policy Research.
E876.R393   1988   327.73—dc 19   87–31958 CIP
ISBN 0–8447–2274–X (pbk. : alk. paper)

AEI Forum 67

© 1987 by the American Enterprise Institute for Public
Policy Research, Washington, D.C. All rights reserved. No
part of this publication may be used or reproduced in any
manner whatsoever without permission in writing from the
American Enterprise Institute except in the case of brief
quotations embodied in news articles, critical articles, or
reviews.

The views expressed in the publications of the American
Enterprise Institute are those of the authors and do not
necessarily reflect the views of the staff, advisory panels,
officers, or trustees of AEI.

"American Enterprise Institute" and (ⒶⒺⒾ) are registered
service marks of the American Enterprise Institute for
Public Policy Research.

Printed in the United States of America

327.73
R287

207469

Participants

CHRISTOPHER C. DEMUTH, president, American Enterprise Institute for Public Policy Research

OWEN HARRIES, AEI adjunct scholar and co-editor of *The National Interest*

IRVING KRISTOL, AEI senior fellow and co-editor of *The Public Interest*

JOSHUA MURAVCHIK, AEI resident scholar and author of *The Uncertain Crusade: Jimmy Carter and the Dilemmas of Human Rights Policy* and "Maximum Feasible Containment," June 1987, in *The New Republic*

STEPHEN ROSENFELD, deputy editorial page editor and columnist, *Washington Post*

STEPHEN SOLARZ (Democrat, New York), chairman, Subcommittee on Asian and Pacific Affairs of the House Foreign Affairs Committee

5.95

The American Enterprise Institute for Public Policy Research

Board of Trustees

Willard C. Butcher, *Chairman*
Chm. and CEO
Chase Manhattan Bank

Paul F. Oreffice, *Vice-Chm.*
Chm. and CEO
Dow Chemical Co.

W. Wallace Abbott
Senior Vice President
Procter & Gamble Co.

Robert Anderson
Chm. and CEO
Rockwell International Corp.

H. Brewster Atwater, Jr.
Chm. and CEO
General Mills, Inc.

Warren L. Batts
Chm. and CEO
Premark International

Winton M. Blount
Chm. and CEO
Blount, Inc.

Edwin L. Cox
Chairman,
Cox Oil & Gas, Inc.

John J. Creedon
Pres. and CEO
Metropolitan Life Insurance Co.

Christopher C. DeMuth
President
American Enterprise Institute

Charles T. Fisher III
Chm. and Pres.
National Bank of Detroit

D. Gale Johnson
Chairman
AEI Council of Academic
  Advisers

George M. Keller
Chm. and CEO
Chevron Corp.

Ben F. Love
Chm. and CEO
Texas Commerce Bancshares, Inc.

Richard B. Madden
Chm. and CEO
Potlatch Corp.

Founded in 1943, AEI is a nonpartisan, nonprofit, research and educational organization based in Washington, D.C. The Institute sponsors research, conducts seminars and conferences, and publishes books and periodicals.

AEI's research is carried out under three major programs: Economic Policy Studies; Foreign Policy and National Security Studies; and Social and Political Studies. The resident scholars and fellows listed in these pages are part of a network that also includes ninety adjunct scholars at leading universities throughout the United States and in several foreign countries.

The views expressed in AEI publications are those of the authors and do not necessarily reflect the views of the staff, advisory panels, officers, or trustees. AEI itself takes no positions on public policy issues.

Robert H. Malott
Chm. and CEO
FMC Corp.

Paul W. McCracken
Edmund Ezra Day University
  Professor Emeritus
University of Michigan

Randall Meyer
President
Exxon Co., U.S.A.

Paul A. Miller
Chm. and CEO
Pacific Lighting Corp.

Richard M. Morrow
Chm. and CEO
Amoco Corp.

James E. Olson
Chm. and CEO
AT&T

David Packard
Chairman
Hewlett-Packard Co.

Charles W. Parry
Director
Aluminum Co. of America

Edmund T. Pratt, Jr.
Chm. and CEO
Pfizer, Inc.

Mark Shepherd, Jr.
Chairman
Texas Instruments, Inc.

Roger B. Smith
Chm. and CEO
General Motors Corp.

Richard D. Wood
Chairman of the Board
Eli Lilly and Co.

Walter B. Wriston
Former Chairman
Citicorp

Officers

Christopher C. DeMuth
President

David B. Gerson
Executive Vice President

James F. Hicks
Vice President, Finance and
  Administration; Treasurer; and
  Secretary

Patrick Ford
Vice President, Public Affairs

Council of Academic Advisers

D. Gale Johnson, *Chairman*
Eliakim Hastings Moore
  Distinguished Service Professor
  of Economics
University of Chicago

Paul M. Bator
John P. Wilson Professor of Law
University of Chicago

Gary S. Becker
University Professor of Economics
  and Sociology
University of Chicago

Donald C. Hellmann
Professor of Political Science and
  International Studies
University of Washington

Gertrude Himmelfarb
Distinguished Professor of
  History
 City University of New York

Nelson W. Polsby
Professor of Political Science
University of California at
  Berkeley

Herbert Stein
A. Willis Robertson
  Professor of Economics
  Emeritus
University of Virginia

Murray L. Weidenbaum
Mallinckrodt Distinguished
  University Professor
Washington University

James Q. Wilson
James Collins Professor of
  Management
University of California at
  Los Angeles

Research Staff

Claude E. Barfield
Resident Fellow; Director,
  Science and Technology

Walter Berns
Adjunct Scholar

Douglas J. Besharov
Resident Scholar; Director,
  Social Responsibility Project

Nicholas N. Eberstadt
Visiting Scholar

Gerald R. Ford
Distinguished Fellow

Murray F. Foss
Visiting Scholar

Suzanne Garment
Resident Scholar

Allan Gerson
Resident Scholar

Robert A. Goldwin
Resident Scholar; Codirector,
  Constitution Project

Gottfried Haberler
Resident Scholar

William S. Haraf
J. Edward Lundy Visiting Scholar;
Director, Financial Markets
  Regulation Project

Karlyn H. Keene
Resident Fellow; Managing
  Editor, *Public Opinion*

Jeane J. Kirkpatrick
Senior Fellow
Counselor to the President for
  Foreign Policy Studies

Marvin H. Kosters
Resident Scholar; Director,
  Economic Policy Studies

Irving Kristol
Senior Fellow

S. Robert Lichter
DeWitt Wallace Fellow

Chong-Pin Lin
Associate Director,
  China Studies Program

John H. Makin
Resident Scholar; Director,
  Fiscal Policy Studies

Brian F. Mannix
Resident Fellow; Managing
  Editor, *Regulation*

Constantine C. Menges
Resident Scholar

Joshua Muravchik
Resident Scholar

Michael Novak
George F. Jewett Scholar;
Director, Social and Political
  Studies

Norman J. Ornstein
Resident Scholar

Richard N. Perle
Resident Fellow

Thomas Robinson
Director, China
  Studies Program

William A. Schambra
Resident Fellow; Codirector,
  Constitution Project

William Schneider
Resident Fellow

Herbert Stein
Senior Fellow;
  Editor, *AEI Economist*

Edward Styles
Director, Publications

Sir Alan Walters
Senior Fellow

Ben J. Wattenberg
Senior Fellow;
  Coeditor, *Public Opinion*

Carolyn L. Weaver
Resident Scholar; Editor,
  Regulation

John C. Weicher
F.K. Weyerhaeuser Scholar

Makoto Yokoyama
Visiting Fellow

CHRISTOPHER C. DeMUTH, president, American Enterprise Institute: The five speakers at this symposium have all written recently on the Reagan Doctrine—some before and some after the revelations we now call the Iran-contra affair.

We will begin with Joshua Muravchik, who is a resident scholar at the American Enterprise Institute, the author of *The Uncertain Crusade: Jimmy Carter and the Dilemmas of Human Rights Policy* and of an article on the Reagan Doctrine in the June 1, 1987, issue of *The New Republic*, "Maximum Feasible Containment." He will be followed by Representative Stephen Solarz, chairman of the Subcommittee on Asian and Pacific Affairs of the House Foreign Affairs Committee and author of "When to Intervene," in the summer 1986 issue of *Foreign Policy*. Next will be Owen Harries, coeditor of *The National Interest,* and an adjunct scholar at AEI and at the Heritage Foundation. Stephen Rosenfeld is the deputy editorial page editor and a columnist for the *Washington Post* and the author of "The Guns of July," an article in the spring 1986 issue of *Foreign Affairs*. Finally, we will hear from Irving Kristol, senior fellow at AEI, coeditor of *The Public Interest,* and publisher of *The National Interest*.

JOSHUA MURAVCHIK, American Enterprise Institute: Although the world is full of problems, there is one

1

central or overarching threat to U.S. security. That is the threat posed by the Soviet Union, which is the only power with the ability, physically, to destroy us. That threat is not something we have imagined, nor is it something of our own making. Indeed, we came to recognize it only reluctantly, following World War II, after having nourished the hope that our Soviet ally in the war would remain our partner in peace. Soviet actions soon proved that hope to be naïve. All evidence since shows that the Soviets continue to see their power and ours as being in conflict. Although they wish to avoid war with us, they intend to continue to expand their empire and their influence, and they hope, eventually, to achieve a position of global pre-eminence.

The conflict that this imposes on us has a dual character. It is a struggle between the world's two foremost military powers. It is also a struggle between two contrasting visions of the future of mankind.

The two superpowers are also the two original models for these contrasting visions. Each of them was founded on an idea, the democratic idea on the one hand and the Communist idea on the other. Each of these is a universal idea, whose claim to validity rests on premises about the very nature of man or of history. These two components of the U.S.-Soviet conflict—the power struggle and the ideological struggle—are inextricably entwined. We may distinguish them, analytically, but in practice we cannot separate them.

The growth of Soviet power reinforces its central ideological claim, the claim to represent an inevitable future. Conversely, the expansion of Soviet power, or of the Soviet empire, although it has always been accomplished by brute force, has always been abetted by political and ideological work designed to paralyze or weaken any resistance.

Upon first recognizing the threat posed by the Soviet Union, the United States responded with a policy of containment. This policy aimed to resist Soviet expansion everywhere but in a strictly defensive manner. Conservative writer James Burnham objected at the time that any strictly defensive strategy was doomed to failure. His objections were anticipated, however, by George Kennan, who had articulated the strategy of containment. Kennan replied, cogently, by turning Lenin's theory of imperialism back on the Soviet Union.

Soviet society, said Kennan, "is rent by internal contradictions," which would lead to its transformation unless it had the opportunity to find outlet through external expansion. Therefore, if we could only "bottle up" the Soviet Union, we would induce in it a fundamental change, or at least a profound mellowing of its system. And, said Kennan, this would occur within ten years.

A fair case can be made that Kennan was vindicated. Stalin's raw terror gave way to Khrushchev's liberal rule, in little more than the decade that Kennan had set out as his time frame. But Khrushchev's rule also showed that an internal mellowing of the Soviet system did not necessarily bring about an abatement of the system's appetite for expansion.

This took the force out of Kennan's reply to Burnham. A policy that was strictly defensive and that had to endure in perpetuity was indeed doomed to failure. Containment, in that sense, continued living on borrowed time, until it finally expired on the battlefields of Vietnam, the quintessential containment war, both in the motives for our entry into it and in the strictly defensive ground rules under which we fought it.

After containment our next effort to work out a response to the central threat we faced was detente, a policy that aimed to enmesh the Soviet Union in a web of relationships that would induce it to contain itself. But the Soviets announced, from the very start of detente—indeed, Chairman Brezhnev himself said it—that detente did not entail a cessation of Soviet support for struggles of national liberation. That is the Soviets' lingo for struggles to extend their empire, just as today they describe what they are doing in Afghanistan as lending fraternal support to the struggle for national liberation by the Afghan people.

After detente we had the policies of Jimmy Carter, perhaps best described as a more conciliatory version of detente. Where Kissinger had sought to influence the Soviets with a policy of carrots and sticks, Carter offered carrots and more carrots. But in the end, after the invasion of Afghanistan had left his policy a shambles, Carter confessed that he had misread Soviet goals.

After Carter came Reagan and the Reagan Doctrine, a name given not by Reagan himself, but by essayist Charles Krauthammer in an effort to give coherent description to a policy that Reagan seems rather to have stumbled into. It was, however, a natural and almost inevitable step in our quest as a nation for a response to the central challenge posed by Soviet power. Since the Soviets will not cease pressing forward and seeking to expand their power and since we cannot, or will not, contain them, as Kennan hoped, at every point where they may choose to try to expand, the obvious option left to us is to press back at points of our choosing, where they may be vulnerable, by supporting anti-Communist insurgencies.

If we do this, and at the same time attempt to resist their expansion as much as we can wherever we can, we may yet succeed in holding their power in check. But to succeed, this strategy needs one more component. It cannot be a strategy of sheer power politics.

I agree with Irving Kristol that the ideological battle between freedom and communism will be resolved by power. But the power battle itself may well be resolved by ideological thrusts and parries, which will shape the spirit, the will, the determination, and even the strategy that each side will bring to the battle.

It is often said these days that communism has lost its ideological appeal because fewer foreign revolutionaries look to Moscow as a model, the way, say, the founders of the Sandinista National Liberation Front did. But this misunderstands the issue, because Communists have never come to power anywhere by winning the support of a majority. They achieve their aims by their success in recruiting small numbers of self-sacrificing dedicated cadres, by infiltrating and manipulating broader political movements, and by sowing disunity and pacifism among their opponents.

And these are things that communism has not lost the capacity to do. In fact they are being done very effectively today, one could say, on every continent. And thus, to defend ourselves adequately, the West must wage political battle, exposing the Communist lies, resisting their influence, and foiling their political tactics with political tactics of our own.

Our political struggle will have many components and will address many small or short-term issues, but it must proceed from a central theme or premise.

That premise must be that our way of life is right and good, that it is accessible to others as well, that we do indeed believe that all men are endowed with "unalienable rights," and that we are prepared, and even eager, to do what we can to help people everywhere to vindicate those rights through the development of democratic political institutions.

In sum, I argue to Congressman Solarz and Stephen Rosenfeld, whom with their permission I take to stand for the liberal camp, that it is not sufficient to ad lib a reaction to this situation or that situation, without a strategy for handling the central problem that we face. And I ask, If not the Reagan Doctrine, then what strategy do you propose?

And I argue to Owen Harries and to Irving Kristol, whom again with permission I take to stand for the conservative camp, that we are unlikely to win the power struggle unless we find a way to wage a political, ideological struggle as an integral part of it. And I ask them how else we can do that but by taking the universal quest for democracy as the banner under which we struggle.

REP. STEPHEN SOLARZ (D-N.Y.): In the 1960s and 1970s, one of the major questions confronting those responsible for American foreign policy was whether we should resist national liberation movements around the world. In the 1980s, one of the major questions that confronts the makers of American foreign policy is whether we should assist national liberation movements around the world. I take the Reagan Doctrine to be the ideological response of the current administration to that new challenge.

The great majority of my colleagues in the Congress and the American people would agree that there are indeed times and places where it serves the national interest of the United States to assist liberation movements resisting Communist tyranny in their own countries. But if the Reagan Doctrine is to be interpreted as a kind of ideological imperative that creates a moral obligation, as it were, for our country to provide material assistance to anti-Communist liberation movements wherever they may be around the world, it can only be seen as a manifest absurdity. While there are places where it does serve our interests to provide assistance to those resisting communism, such as Afghanistan, there are clearly circumstances where it does not.

The Reagan administration itself has implicitly rejected the universal formulation of the doctrine to which it has lent its name by virtue of its refusal to provide assistance to Renamo in Mozambique, recognizing that would be counterproductive to some important American interests in southern Africa.

In 1956 and in 1968, both Republican and Democratic administrations concluded that it would not serve the best interests of the United States to provide assistance to the Hungarian freedom fighters and to those striving to bring about democracy in Czechoslovakia, however much we sympathized with the efforts of those peoples to free themselves from the yoke of Communist tyranny. Hypothetically, if one could postulate the emergence of liberation movements in, say, Yugoslavia and China—two Communist but, in a way, anti-Soviet countries—it would clearly not serve our interests to rush to their support. Such support would probably drive the Yugoslavs and the Chinese back into the embrace of the Soviet Union, which, from a geopolitical point of view, would hardly be in the best interests of the United States.

In foreign policy, we ought to be wary of acting on the basis of doctrines that create ideological imperatives with a universal application. Given the complexities of the world in which we live, these grandiose generalizations can often lead us into actions that are insensitive to the complexities of particular situations and that can boomerang instead of promoting our national interests.

I argue for a case-by-case, country-by-country determination of how best to resist communism and promote democracy. Joshua Muravchik asks what is the alternative to the Reagan Doctrine. I would say the alternative to the Reagan Doctrine is the prudent advocacy of democracy and the containment of communism by ways and means to be determined by what will be most effective and most appropriate in any given circumstance. Without being indifferent to the fate of freedom in Nicaragua, for example, one can conclude that it is counterproductive to provide aid to the contras. There are many nations around the world where we try, in a variety of ways—through diplomacy, through the application of economic sanctions, through the instrumentality of the National Endowment for Democracy and the party institutes— to assist those attempting to carve out a greater degree of freedom for themselves. I do not believe that, if we decide not to provide material assistance to liberation movements seeking either to overthrow repressive regimes or to establish democracy through military means, we are therefore indifferent to the fate of freedom in those countries. In some nations, assistance to those seeking by force of arms to change their political circumstances may serve our interests. In other situations, it clearly does not.

We were asked to speak about the Reagan Doctrine after Iran-contra. Of course, Iran-contra has not yet run its course, but it is perhaps not too early to offer some preliminary observations.

Colonel North's impassioned defense of the need for covert operations and for secrecy in the implementation of these operations notwithstanding, most Americans would agree that in the dangerous world in which we do indeed live we cannot afford to tie our hands behind our backs and preclude the possibility of covert operations in any and all circumstances.

There is a fairly strong national consensus that in certain times, circumstances, and occasions, the best interests of the country are served by covert operations. Colonel North's testimony raises, however, the classic dilemma of how we reconcile the necessity for covert action in a dangerous world with the requirements of democracy.

As a result of the investigation of the Church committee, we discovered in the 1970s that when agencies of our government responsible for those operations were left to their own devices and unrestrained by the Congress, they tended to engage in activities that most Americans believed were incompatible with our values and counterproductive to our interests. We discovered that we were attempting to assassinate the heads of state of unfriendly countries, while attempting, through bribery and other means, to bring about the downfall of governments that might have been considered friendly to the United States.

Out of that national debate produced by the revelations concerning the activities of the CIA, a consensus emerged that the way to deal with that problem was not to rule out the possibility of covert operations, but rather to establish a framework within which those actions and activities could be legitimized by our democratic system.

We established two intelligence committees, one in the House and one in the Senate, with a legal requirement that they be notified in a timely fashion before any covert activities were conducted. The theory was that it was probably asking too much to require the executive branch to inform 435 members of the House and 100 members of the Senate about covert activities but that it ought to inform a limited number of members in the House and Senate, whose wisdom, whose experience, whose expertise could be brought to bear on these questions and who could serve as a surrogate for the other members of Congress.

I think that was a reasonable way of reconciling the necessity for covert action with the requirements of democracy. It worked fairly well. Although a leak from these committees may occasionally have compromised our covert activities, many more leaks from the executive branch compromised these activities.

Colonel North testified that he had to make a choice between lies and lives and that he had no alternative but to deceive members of Congress about what we were doing, lest he compromise the objectives of these operations. It seems to me that what he said was not only inconsistent with the law but completely insensitive to the consensus that had emerged in the Congress about how to reconcile these two imperatives.

As a consequence of these hearings, we are likely to get legislation tightening the requirements that the president notify the intelligence committees, making it clear that the timely notice we have in mind is a matter of days rather than months or years. That will be a significant consequence of what we have heard in these hearings.

What we do with respect to Nicaragua is very much up in the air. Colonel North's main motivation seems to have been to engage in arms sales to Iran so that the resources, or the residuals, generated by those sales could be used to help the contras. The Congress is closely divided on this issue, and how it will come out remains to be seen.

But one thing is absolutely clear. Even those who strongly believe we should help the contras and even those who strongly believe Colonel North is a great American patriot are likely to reject the notion that the interests of the United States are served by establishing—as Colonel North, Director Casey, and others seemed to be doing—a kind of secret CIA outside of the CIA. Conducting off-the-shelf covert operations run by people who are unelected and unaccountable, using funds that are unauthorized and unappropriated, is clearly an end run not only around the Congress but around the law. It is inconceivable that the Congress would permit it. If it takes legislation to prevent the establishment of a secret CIA, such legislation would command overwhelming support in the Congress.

One of the things that concerns me the most is that, in the process of attempting to promote democracy abroad, we came perilously close to undermining democracy here at home. If we ever lose our democracy in this country, it will be because of well-meaning people who have convinced themselves that they know better than the elected representatives of the people what the national interest requires.

I can understand why our fellow Americans are so impressed with the seeming patriotism, sincerity, and determination of Colonel North. I am appalled, however, that someone who openly admits to lying, not only to the Congress but to his superiors, who clearly advocated with great passion a policy that constituted bargaining for hostages and selling arms to a terrorist state when we were publicly calling on our friends and allies not to sell arms to such a state, and who participated in an effort to establish a secret CIA to end run congressional restrictions could have won such favor with the American people.

This is utterly unacceptable behavior. If it were carried on consistently by this or any other administration, it would constitute a clear threat to democracy. The successful implementation of our foreign policy—the establishment of a sustained consensus that allows the executive branch to carry out its policy with the support of the American people—requires the trust and confidence of the Congress that the administration is obeying the law of the land.

Whatever momentary advantage an administration may get by deceiving the Congress on one issue is likely to create infinitely greater problems for it on other issues in the future. I think, for example, at least some congressional committees will adopt the practice of putting all administration witnesses under oath. That has not been done in the past. But when deceit and misrepresentation appear to characterize the testimony of administration witnesses before congressional committees when they are not under oath, the Congress is likely to feel that it can get the truth to which it is entitled only by confronting administration witnesses with the possibility of perjury if they continue to deceive the Congress.

OWEN HARRIES, *National Interest:* I've been apparently cast in the role of defender of the Reagan Doctrine today. In fact my position is rather more complicated than that. It is, in sum, that I agree with everything that the proponents of the Reagan Doctrine want to do in practice, the particular policies that they stand for—that is, giving aid to the insurgents or the freedom fighters or, perhaps more accurately, the independence fighters in Nicaragua, Angola, Afghanistan, and Cambodia. But I have serious reservations about formulating these discrete policies into something called the Reagan Doctrine.

It amounts to a serious case of overselling in that it raises unrealizable expectations. It presents easy targets for people like Mr. Rosenfeld, who can simultaneously invite alarm over the scope of the thing and ridicule it for the gap between its pretensions and what it amounts to in fact. It also invites an indiscriminate approach toward what—and here I agree with Mr. Solarz—requires great discrimination. The Reagan Doctrine simply cannot be the centerpiece of American foreign policy, because by its very nature, by its definition, it refers to a few peripheral countries, mostly small ones on the frontier of the Soviet empire. Apart from the countries I've already mentioned, Ethiopia and Mozambique are usually named, and that's all. It has little or nothing to say about the rest of the world, what America should be doing in relation to Europe, to northeast Asia, and to central fronts. It simply is irrelevant to those.

This problem is evident in Josh Muravchik's article in *The New Republic*. After dismissing containment as a collapsed policy, and selective containment as even worse, he finally has to opt for a policy of maximum feasible containment for most of the world, supplemented by the Reagan Doctrine of active defense in a few selected locations.

He is forced to that position because the Reagan

Doctrine simply doesn't fill the gaps elsewhere. So I suggest that it would be better if we declared it a policy but recognized this limitation—that the Reagan Doctrine is, at best, an important subsidiary dimension of U.S. foreign policy. We should adjust its rhetoric accordingly, so that it is less vulnerable to attack.

As with all doctrine, the Reagan Doctrine emphasizes the general at the expense of the particular, ends at the expense of means, consistency at the expense of prudence. Whenever "prudence" appears in Josh's article, it either appears in quotation marks or is described as an empty conservative shibboleth or words to that effect.

Josh is fond of dichotomizing as a polemical technique. He says we have to make a sharp choice between isolationism and the Reagan Doctrine, that nothing else is possible. We have to choose either ideology or power politics. Let me stress that my reservations about doctrines does not mean that I advocate sheer pragmatism or practicalism. Ideas, concepts, principles—call them what you will—are certainly necessary in foreign policy, but they are not sufficient.

The problem with the propagators of this doctrine, as with all other doctrines, is that they emphasize principle heavily and pay little attention to the crucial question of circumstances. But policy is essentially about the interplay of these two. Until the questions of how, when, where, and how much are answered, we won't have a policy. We will simply have a concept. In his *Foreign Policy* article, Mr. Solarz poses six questions: What are America's central policy objectives in the area in question? What is the best way to achieve U.S. objectives? How do America's friends in the region view U.S. support for the insurgency? How closely tied to the Soviet Union is the regime that the insurgency is challenging? How likely are the insurgents to achieve their goals with and without American aid? And would achievement of the resistance's objectives significantly improve life in the country and advance U.S. interests?

These questions are very well posed. They are essential questions that anyone actually shaping or conducting a foreign policy will have to answer. On ideology, I agree very much with Josh's refutations of the view that the ideological battle is won and that Marxism-Leninism is now discredited. That is a half-truth. Marxism-Leninism is discredited as far as economic development is concerned. It is not discredited as an ideology designed to guide, justify, and legitimize the seizure and retention of monopolistic vertical power. As such, it continues to be extremely attractive and useful to third world radical intellectuals. One might put it that Marxism may be dead but Leninism is still selling very well.

I also agree with Josh's view that American policy must employ ideology and fight the ideological war. He put it much better in his comments here than he did in his article. There he seems to draw a sharp distinction between an ideological approach and a power or political approach that simply creates unnecessary and unrealistic problems. That sharp choice doesn't have to be made. What is needed is to combine the two. If anybody in our time, or my time anyway, has proved the possibility of such a combination, it would be, of course, Winston Churchill.

As I have said, Mr. Solarz sets out the general criteria for intervening excellently, but I disagree strongly with the conclusions he reaches in two crucial cases, those of Nicaragua and Angola. He is against military aid and military pressure in both cases. I am for it. Let me speak briefly to that.

On Angola, I don't believe as Mr. Solarz believes that the deal of a South African withdrawal from Namibia in return for a Cuban withdrawal from Angola is available. It is intrinsically unavailable and unrealistic for the simple reason that it would amount to committing suicide by the MPLA government of Angola. It could not exist without the Cuban presence. So any policy based on such a deal is a nonstarter.

And I especially don't think it is a bargain to withdraw from Namibia now in return for promise of withdrawal of the Cubans in three or four or five years. After all, if Senator Biden can change his mind about Robert Bork's appointment to the Supreme Court in six months, so can the MPLA change its mind about the Cubans.

On Nicaragua, Mr. Solarz argues that not overthrowing the Sandinistas but getting them to agree to nonalignment and noninterference should be the goals of American policy. If achieved, that would be enough. This has never been tested, he says, and testing it should be the proper objective of American policy. This turns out to be a red herring, however, because he goes on to say that if it is tested, and if it fails—if the Sandinistas turn down such a deal and turn down the Contadora process—even then, the United States should still not give unilateral aid to the contras. They should instead turn to the Organization of American States with "confidence in a collective response."

Given both the record of the OAS and the nature of American interests in the stability of Central America, this seems to me to be feeble in the extreme. Central

America is so important that the Nicaraguan question should be taken out of the context of the Reagan Doctrine altogether and treated as a special case on its own merits. It is too important to be discussed simply in terms of generally promoting democracy. It is too important to be discussed in terms of leading the Soviet Union at the "margin," which is how the Reagan Doctrine policy is sometimes put and defended. The United States has a vital interest in the stability of Central America, and it needs no justification beyond that.

Briefly, then, my conclusions are that I am critical of Josh Muravchik's position on general theoretical or conceptual grounds but agree on the practical policies that he advocates. There is need for a rhetoric more attuned to what a policy of active defense can actually mean. It is a case, as somebody said, of raise the bridge or lower the water. I agree with Mr. Solarz's general statement, to a considerable extent, of the sort of criteria that are required when one takes up the question of whether to intervene or not, but I disagree on specific policies in those two key cases of Nicaragua and Angola.

I haven't addressed the question of the hearings because it seems to me that this forum was conceived when they indicated that the support for intervention was being seriously undermined and probably destroyed by the impact of the Iran-contra affair. As events have shown, this can turn around. These hearings could strengthen that basis. We just don't know. We don't know what will happen at the end of next week when other people have testified. As for Colonel North, Morton Kondracke suggested that he should be packed off to the Marines again. I don't think that. He should be kept in the foreign policy industry but should be switched from the manufacturing division to marketing.

STEPHEN ROSENFELD, *Washington Post:* Some of us are transfixed by the specter of the Soviet Union pressing forward at every point. We are also inspired by the universality of the values of democracy. We want to fine-tune the Reagan Doctrine on the basis of our six, seven, eight years' experience with it. Some of us would like to turn down the rhetoric. I would like to see a Reagan Doctrine shorn of rhetoric and wonder if that isn't some kind of oxymoron.

I am more transfixed by the spectacle of the U.S. government coming undone, of the Reagan administration coming undone, of the capacity and standing of our country being seen to be in some confusion and disarray, not fatal, but embarrassing. Against those who would concentrate on the international environment, I would concentrate more on the domestic policy environment.

I would like to suggest a few of the things we've learned about the Reagan Doctrine in the past few years. It is not easy to sustain a policy that has the aspect of a doctrine, which suggests a consistency and a demand for self-discipline that are not easily worked up and are not easily sustained in our society. I put that forward as a proposition that doesn't need too much argument.

More serious, there is some confusion, which is not always identified as confusion, about the source of the Reagan Doctrine—whether it emanates from some conception of our national interest to which one can say yes or no; whether it emanates from some conception of our ideals and their universality, something we have seen in Oliver North that allows any one of us to become the spokesman; or whether the doctrine emanates from some concept of majority will, which is one of the subthemes of the Oliver North testimony and which one can hear from the president of the United States on various days, when he says, let the people decide.

It introduces a particularly troublesome element when we're dealing with an issue on which the last president changed his mind once or twice, on which the Congress has changed its mind at least three times so far in this administration and may be about to change it a fourth. The language of legislation such as the Boland Amendment makes it exceedingly difficult to say, over a period of time, what is the majority will, even of Congress. Public opinion polls reflect, according to one set of numbers, a distaste for certain types of American intervention including the intervention in Nicaragua. In other words, when one starts to say that the Reagan Doctrine is somehow dictated by the popular will, one arrives at some very difficult problems of definition that have not been resolved.

In addition to my observations on the difficulty of sustaining a policy that is a doctrine and on the question of the sources of the Reagan Doctrine, our experience also enlightens us as to the difficulties involved in the essential component of the policy—its secrecy. Our system has difficulty dealing with secrecy, which puts great temptations in the hands of presidents and others. This goes to the heart of the dilemma of an open society being run in a dangerous world, as Oliver North seems to think he's the first to understand.

Those of us who have reservations like mine about the Reagan Doctrine are taxed, and not unfairly, by my colleague Joshua Muravchik for ad libbing, for having no strategy. The question is asked, If not the Reagan Doctrine, then what? A reasonable question, which I will answer with three points.

First, preemptive diplomacy. The Reagan Doctrine is usually applied in places where the Soviets surged in the 1970s while we were distracted by Vietnam or something else. Or they are described as situations where economic and social conditions have ripened. But why not describe them as situations where American policy or Western policy failed or was distracted or did poorly? Who will say that our handling of Iran and Nicaragua in the 1970s did not contribute to the denouements there, which gave us so much trouble?

In this Reagan period—in Asia particularly, but not only there—we have had some remarkable and cheering examples. Call it luck, call it preemptive diplomacy, call it a little bit of a helping hand or whatever, we have seen situations that could have gone rotten turn a little toward the sun. Let's hope it continues. But why wait until everything collapses and then invent a doctrine that is a mop-up doctrine, the Reagan Doctrine? Let's be on our toes. That's number one.

Second, I guess I'd stand still for a little ad libbing, policy ad libbing, although I could think of something more dignified to call it. Mr. Harries is prepared to be intelligent about picking our spots and to conduct argument about it. I like that. Sometimes the notion is that the thermostats of critics of the Reagan Doctrine are not set high enough to allow them into the control room. I won't defend myself against that charge. In picking our spots, we should do it far from the American news media, far from public scrutiny. We should do it in Afghanistan and not in Nicaragua, because people who believe enough to fight for their freedom will do it in ways they find necessary. It may not pass the scrutiny of people like me or others.

Third, in raising questions about the Reagan Doctrine, don't look always, and only, at the international environment. Look at the domestic consensus. That is a better standard for policy as our policy wars have shown us over the past twenty years than is the standard of ideological consistency. And keep in mind, too, that the domestic consensus must cover not only the ends of policy but the means.

IRVING KRISTOL, American Enterprise Institute: I don't know what the Reagan Doctrine is. There's a Muravchik Doctrine with which I don't quite agree. There's a Kristol Doctrine to which I give cautious approval. But what Ronald Reagan means by his doctrine, he hasn't told us yet. Maybe he hasn't yet received a memo on it.

The most important aspect of the Reagan Doctrine is negative—namely, it is witness to the fact that certain guiding ideas of American foreign policy in the past forty years are no longer alive and valid. Josh Muravchik has mentioned those ideas.

The fact that there is such a doctrine, that even someone like Congressman Solarz does not reject it entirely but only dislikes its implementations, means that the idea of a liberal internationalism, for instance, of subordinating American foreign policy to the authority of international organizations, is dead. It still survives in the State Department, but that's what state departments are for. They're museums of dead ideas.

The idea of containment is also dead for the reason that Josh Muravchik pointed out. It has been a long time since we first had that idea. It just hasn't worked very well.

The idea of detente is dead for the same reason. It just didn't work very well. The Soviets do not get enmeshed in webs of economic and diplomatic relations that result in some fundamental change in their foreign policy. They just refuse to get enmeshed—that's all.

The idea of a balance of power as a guiding idea for American foreign policy, in my opinion, was never a serious contender. It is too clearly irrelevant in an ideological conflict between two major powers. The idea of the balance of power, which took shape in the eighteenth century, emerged precisely to end ideological conflicts, specifically the religious wars between Protestants and Catholics. In such an ideological conflict, the idea of the balance of power is not irrelevant—it is just that the idea is always likely to be subordinated to large goals. If either party or both parties should be interested in an imbalance of power, we do not get a balance of power. It is obvious that the Soviets cannot help but strive for such an imbalance, and it is not clear that American democracy could calmly accept any such balance for long.

The main contribution of the so-called Reagan Doctrine is that it leaves the door open to some perhaps creative thinking about American foreign policy. As Josh says, we do have an ideological conflict between all Communist regimes and the American and other Western democracies. They say so. We say so, or we should say so. That's a fact.

This imposes upon us certain obligations—namely, to speak out about our ideals and ideas and to expose the falsity of their ideals and ideas. This latter is especially important. The ideological debate between democracy and totalitarian socialism, if that's the way it is defined, is a very peculiar debate in which the other side has all the advantages. The other side offers an ideal vision of the future. All we have to offer is the present. It is very easy for an ideal vision of the future to be superior to any mere actuality.

That is why our ideological defense of American democracy tends not to be persuasive to people all over the world. We go around telling them how good America is, and they look at America. Yes, it's good in some ways, not so good in other ways. We rather like it; they may or may not. It's hard to persuade them that our way of life is something they should cherish, that this is something they should feel strongly about. A Socialist ideal, however, is very, very attractive, particularly to people who see themselves as having high positions in a future Socialist society, as most Socialist activists do.

So, it is a debate in which we begin with a disadvantage. Our prodemocratic propaganda has very little effect in fact. Our anti-Communist propaganda does have some effect because the reality can be compared with the ideal. More and more people, looking at the Soviet Union, at Cuba, and at other countries, are becoming persuaded that democracy may not be as wonderful as Mr. Reagan claims, but nevertheless is preferable.

Not much is to be gained in pretending that we can have a "crusade for democracy" at the ideological level. Democracy in the United States? Well, what you see is what you get. That's our democracy. While people may have no illusions about the reality—I mean, there's no desire to emigrate to the Soviet Union—they still can be very anti-American. I have many acquaintances in England—professors, you know—

23

ALBRIGHT COLLEGE LIBRARY 207469

who are always anti-American and if not pro-Soviet at least anti-anti-Communist. Nevertheless, they come to this country to accept professorships. This does not affect their belief that anti-Soviet propaganda is probably exaggerated.

We also have this disadvantage in the ideological conflict. I think it is insurmountable and will remain as long as the political mode of thinking in the world is as utopian as it has been in the twentieth century. Once the world becomes deutopianized—and that, indeed, would be a wonderful prospect—we would not need any propaganda. People would look at the United States, at the Soviet Union, and would see what they would see, and they would understand.

Nevertheless, there is something that has to be done in this area. This regime has to articulate its ideals and its ideas. It should do so modestly. It should do so unapologetically, with self-confidence. But it should not do so in a crusading vein.

It should also permit this ideology, to some degree, to influence its diplomacy. Diplomacy, unlike foreign policy, is to some degree in the realm of freedom, not the realm of necessity. Diplomacy involves words more than deeds. There is no reason why we should not make our views on certain matters clear. We should make clear our disapproval of specific actions by other governments, hostile or friendly. If we have an authoritarian ally, we have to say we have an authoritarian ally, not pretend that it is a democratic ally, and we should explain why it is useful to us, or necessary to us, to have an authoritarian ally. We should not pretend in our foreign policy statements that we can look forward in the near future to democracy conquering the world. The world is not like that. I am not one of those who is thrilled by the success of democracy in Argentina or in the Philippines or, imminently, in Korea. I am a betting man, and I will lay odds that democracy will not survive in those countries. The preconditions of democracy are complex—certain strong cultural traditions, certain strong cultural attitudes. So far as I can see, those countries do not have them, and therefore, a democracy in any of them would shortly be discredited and be replaced by some sort of authoritarian regime of either the left or the right. That is apparently their norm, and I refuse to feel guilty about it. I refuse to say, "We failed in the Philippines," because the Filipinos cannot govern themselves, as they cannot, in my opinion. Neither have the Argentines been able to govern themselves since they became an independent nation, 175 years ago or so.

The other part of the Reagan Doctrine, or the Muravchik Doctrine, or my doctrine, is the question of action. What do we do in this ideological conflict, as distinct from what we say? Here we run into problems if we paint with too broad a brush, as I think Josh does. He talks about being a sponsor of revolutions. Against whom? Against friendly authoritarian governments, or only against Communist regimes? If we take the latter line, we will properly be accused of hypocrisy. I don't believe we should be a sponsor of revolutions, except under very special circumstances.

We will surely not sponsor revolution in Eastern Europe. In a nuclear world, that is far too dangerous. We will not do it unless we indulge in a brazen Machiavellian calculation that we have to do it in order to get the Soviet Union to desist from doing something elsewhere. Thus we might provoke rebellions in Eastern Europe in order to prevent the Soviets from doing something in the Western Hemisphere. That is hard to imagine, but who knows? That would be cold-blooded Machiavellianism, something to be undertaken with great reluctance. If absolutely necessary, we would do it. But we should not sponsor revolutions against authoritarian governments simply because they are not democratic. Not every people in the world is capable of self-government. We hope that they all will be eventually. That is the American dream, but there's no rush. It could take a very long time, and the dream may turn out to be wrong. We shall see.

My version of the Reagan Doctrine makes a fairly clear distinction between diplomacy and foreign policy. We should use our diplomatic influence, obviously, to push the actions of other nations into a closer congruence with our ideals. In human rights, for instance, we can do a little, and should—but the effects are likely to be marginal and may even turn out to be counterproductive. There are limits to what we can do in other countries. American foreign policy toward Turkey should not be determined by the way Turks treat their prisoners, political or criminal. Turks have never been famous for treating their prisoners in a kind and gentle way. We should make it clear to the world that we would prefer more humane treatment of prisoners in Turkey, but nothing beyond that should play a role in our policy toward Turkey.

In the world of action, we are constrained to do what the Soviet Union does, to the degree that we can do it, though not necessarily using the same means. There is always a degree of symmetry between the actions of great powers because foreign policy is not the realm of freedom: it is the realm of necessity.

Most of the time, circumstances out of our control shape what can be done. On intervention, Mr. Solarz's points are, on the whole, valid. I think they were better expressed by John Stuart Mill in 1859, in his essay on nonintervention, when Russia, of all countries, in that year invaded Hungary, of all countries, and the British got very excited about it. Mill said that it is desirable for great powers not to intervene in the internal affairs of smaller powers. But if one power intervenes, then another power has the right to intervene. Whether it would be prudent to intervene is a question of circumstance.

There may even be extreme circumstances where we have a right to intervene on purely moral grounds. If the smaller country over which we have preponderant power started committing genocide, for example, we would have a moral right to intervene, though we might not. We did not, after all, intervene in Cambodia.

And so the right of intervention can be modified or canceled by prudential considerations. The Soviet Union believes it has the right to intervene anywhere, any time it's convenient. That is part of its Marxist-Leninist doctrine. It doesn't believe in the principle of nonintervention, and since it does not, neither can we. All we can do is, like the Soviets, be guided by the specific realities involving intervention in particular cases and in particular circumstances.

As I said, we are not going to intervene in any significant way in Eastern Europe except for Machiavellian purposes, which I hope never come to pass. The future of Eastern Europe will be determined by future developments within the Soviet Union. We have very little control over these developments, and we should tell the East Europeans this, while at the same time expressing our sympathy, encouraging them in their hope of eventual freedom, even printing their *samizdat*, smuggling Bibles into the Soviet Union or into Eastern Europe, and the like. That is fine. But we will never intervene in any military way to liberate Eastern Europe. The Soviets have made it clear that Eastern Europe is what the French call their *glacis*. That is, it's their buffer area, and any effort by any one of those countries to become an ally of the United States would be regarded as a threat to their national security.

How do we respond? We respond by saying, if that's the way they are going to go about things, we have to go about them in a similar way. We should have a revised Monroe Doctrine in the Western Hemisphere. What applies to Eastern Europe in their case should certainly apply to the Western Hemisphere in our case. The Western Hemisphere is our *glacis*. We should not accept a Communist government allied, economically or militarily, to the Soviet Union in the Western Hemisphere. We might accept a "Finlandized" government, just as the Soviet Union has accepted a capitalist and relatively democratic Finland. We might accept it. But Finland does not get economic aid from the United States. Finland has no military ties to the United States. Finland is very cautious in what it does about the Soviet Union.

In the case of Nicaragua, we ought to be willing to accept such a solution. But Nicaragua could not accept that solution. The Sandinistas could not because the regime could not survive without Soviet support, economic and military. Once it became clear that the Sandinistas would not Finlandize themselves, we should not have established the contras. We should have invaded. We should have given the Sandinistas an ultimatum: You have ten days to make up your mind—either you Finlandize yourself or we invade.

28

Then we should have invaded. The president has, I believe, sixty days in which to notify Congress. By that point Nicaragua would have been occupied, the regime would have fallen, and then there would have been congressional hearings.

The American people would have supported the president. The American people always rally behind the president when he makes a successful invasion.

On supporting the contras, obviously I now support them since we did not do what we should have done. But the fact is that we are no good at sponsoring and conducting guerrilla insurrections. Many Americans will be quick to point out that guerrilla insurrections involve violations of the principles of the American Civil Liberties Union. It is not liberals who lead or make guerrilla insurrections. A lot of thugs get involved in guerrilla warfare. A lot of inhumane things are done. A lot of innocent people are killed. That is the nature of guerrilla insurrections, sponsored by anyone.

Our political system finds it difficult to cope with a guerrilla insurrection that involves what is involved in Sri Lanka or in Peru or in Nicaragua or in El Salvador—namely, a ruthless and rather brutal attempt to subvert and overthrow the regime. If we support such an insurrection, then we have to say we are going to support it and if innocent people are killed, that is part of the game. It does not pose a moral issue to us. How we can do that, I don't know. I'm not sure Congress would accept that. I'm not sure the media would accept that. I'm not sure the American people would accept that.

In general, where appropriate, I prefer direct American intervention in which we can be pretty efficient if we go about it in a whole-hearted way, as against sponsoring guerrilla insurrections that get us involved in what most people would regard as moral dilemmas. That's my "Kristol" version of the Reagan Doctrine. I haven't yet put it into memo form, and I doubt very much that the American government will accept it when I do. I think we will continue to go on two tracks—a high-level track of fine-sounding words and a low-level track of adapting, in a bumbling way, to the realities of international affairs—and that will create enormous tensions in our society.

MR. DEMUTH: Beginning with Josh Muravchik, each member of the panel will now have the opportunity to add brief additional comments. Then I will call for questions from the floor.

MR. MURAVCHIK: I would like to select one point of dispute with each of the other panelists, if I can do it quickly, with an apology to Congressman Solarz because he's not here to defend himself.

He expresses, in essence, very little disagreement with me, although he doesn't quite answer the question that I put. What is the overall strategic concept? Although he offers an interesting argument about the conditions for backing anti-Communist insurrections in the article to which Owen Harries referred, it does not come to grips with the central problem, nor does it state plainly what I think really motivates him. He embraces the resistance movements in Afghanistan and Cambodia but rejects those in Angola and Nicaragua. Can he make a case in terms of many of the criteria set forth in his *Foreign Policy* article that the former are more worthy of support than the latter? Whatever the depredations of the Nicaraguan contras or the ideological twists and turns of Jonas Savimbi in Angola, they are certainly no further from our ideals than are the Afghan Mujahadeen or than are a major component of the Cambodian rebels who are fighting against the Vietnamese—those who adhere to Pol Pot.

His unarticulated premise, I believe, is that Afghanistan and Cambodia are all right because those are both cases of supporting a nationalist movement resisting a foreign invasion. Angola, which is more ambiguous, and Nicaragua, which is quite clear-cut, are not all right because those are questions of lending support to an insurrection seeking to overthrow an indigenous Communist government. That is the step that Congressman Solarz and many of those who have argued along similar lines are unwilling to take. In my conception, that is the essential step.

To Owen Harries, I myself didn't choose the name Reagan Doctrine and wouldn't have. Reagan is a phenomenon of limited duration, but I hope this policy will not be. And "doctrine" does imply a certain rigidity that is completely unnecessary and invites semantic arguments. I would much rather call this a policy of "engagement" or some other such term, just as the "Truman Doctrine" eventually gave way to the term "containment."

Further, it is quite true that although I wish to go beyond containment, I favor pursuing containment as far as we can. But the essential point is that since we are not willing to do what Kennan once proposed, which is to try to stop Soviet or Communist expansion everywhere, and since the Soviets won't stop themselves, then we have to wrestle with this bear. We cannot wrestle by the self-imposed rule that whatever territory is not theirs is up for grabs, but whatever they have is sacrosanct and we won't touch it. And that is the central argument I want to make.

MR. KRISTOL: What you're talking about is the anti-Brezhnev doctrine.

MR. MURAVCHIK: That's exactly right. To Steve Rosenfeld, let me just take issue with you on a key part of your response to my question about an alternative, which is what you called preemptive diplomacy.

In every situation to which the so-called Reagan Doctrine is now applied—that is, every situation where there is now an anti-Communist insurgency—we indeed tried preventive diplomacy, and it failed because diplomacy devoid of force to back it up just didn't work.

We scurried all around Nicaragua in the last year, at least, trying to get Somoza out, eventually getting Somoza out and getting a resolution from the OAS that called for his withdrawal in exchange for certain commitments from the Sandinistas to create a democratic, pluralist, nonaligned government. We got a letter from the junta named by the Sandinistas promising that they in fact would do this. On that basis Somoza left, and the transfer of power to the Sandinistas was effectuated. But because there was no willingness to use American force to enforce those promises, the preventive diplomacy was of no value whatsoever. The agreement that the Sandinistas made was just tossed aside as so much paper.

In Angola, there was also an agreement that we diplomatically encouraged between the three liberation forces—at that time the MPLA, FLNA, and UNITA—for power sharing and democratic transition. It was a beautiful agreement—only the MPLA and the Soviets and the Cubans decided to make so much paper of it. Once our Congress, with the Clark Amendment, decreed that we would not resist by force, or aid those who wanted to resist by force, then our preventive diplomacy was of no value whatsoever. Similar things could be said about the diplomacy of Indochina, which on paper led to a denouement different from what we have had.

Finally, to Irving Kristol, I would quarrel with your belief that the ideological struggle between democracy and communism is stacked against us. You yourself gave a hint of the evidence to the contrary when you pointed out the vast attraction of the United States to immigrants, not just to British professors but to people from all walks of life and all parts of the world. From recent reports, there is no parallel immigration crisis in the Soviet Union or in any of the other "workers' paradises."

In events throughout Latin America, in the Philippines, in Korea, in India, and in lots of other places in the past decade, we see a vast amount of evidence that democracy is enormously more appealing than any dictatorial alternative.

The difficulty—which differs from the one you stated—is that to create and preserve a democracy requires not just a small number of supporters of democracy. It requires a fairly widespread consensus that this is the right set of rules, that people will play by those rules, and that they will act with restraint if they lose under those rules. Imposing totalitarianism or other forms of tyranny does not require such a widespread consensus. It can often be done with a small band of individuals at strategic points.

Democracy does have a disadvantage against its enemies in the realm of sheer power politics, but in the ideological realm it has a tremendous advantage. That is the advantage we must employ precisely because it is a counterweight against the disadvantages we suffer vis-à-vis totalitarianism.

MR. HARRIES: I am a bit worried by the way both Josh Muravchik and Irving Kristol dismiss all these past policies rather cavalierly. Containment is finished, liberal internationalism is finished, detente is finished, balance of power is finished.

One cannot proceed in those terms. This way of going on says more about the way intellectuals think about foreign policy than about what is really possible. That is, they tend to be bewitched by labels and by the need for clarity and consistency and for the idea to inform the policy.

The actual situation is necessarily much more messy than that. We will always have a mixture of all these. We will always have to resort to various ingredients of all these policy approaches to cope with the world. There are elements of detente and of containment still operative, and as far as I can see there almost always will be. Josh's article points to this fact.

I don't know whether Irving is right in saying that it is invasion or nothing, virtually, whenever we are faced with a problem country. America is no good at supporting insurrections, but it had better get good at supporting insurrections, because there aren't all that many Grenadas around that can be done in a weekend. Nicaragua could not have been done that quickly and held together afterward.

We had a dramatic exhibition in Oliver North's testimony last week of what can be done in the process of educating. Those possibilities should be fully explored to find out what can be done over a period, in a sustained way, without depending on the conviction, the passion, and the impact of one man.

Mr. Solarz was eloquent in the last part of what he said on the problem of lying to the American people. The whole question of truth telling has now assumed the quality of an absolute moral imperative in American public life.

If that is truly the case, I suggest that the present state of affairs is unsatisfactory. We should do it properly. Truth telling should apply, not merely to one arm of the American government, but to the whole of the system—in particular to that part Mr. Solarz belongs to. The legislature should be held to the same standard in the same way as the executive arm is, if only as an exercise in *reductio ad absurdum*. It would be healthy to ask them to apply to themselves the test they apply to others and bring home to them what is involved in these absolute standards.

MR. ROSENFELD: I'll simply associate myself, with pleasure, with Owen Harries's criticisms of Irving Kristol, who seems to think we can snap our fingers and have everything come out right. His indifference to the ways and the protocols of Washington is exceeded only by Oliver North's.

MR. KRISTOL: I was just wondering whether it's exceeded by Ollie North's, or not.

The important thing to say about the Reagan Doctrine, whatever it means, is that it does signify the rejection of the Brezhnev Doctrine. We do not accept the fact that a Communist regime, once established, is safe forever from hostile efforts on our part. That is the minimal statement of the Reagan Doctrine, and it is an important statement.

On the question of immigration, yes, of course, everyone knows that people would prefer to come to the United States and not go to the Soviet Union. The trouble is, we can't let them all in. We could end the rebellion in El Salvador tomorrow by simply making Salvador an associated commonwealth like Puerto Rico, declaring all Salvadorans American citizens, and saying, Come on in, if you want. We'd then import the rebels, and we wouldn't have to suppress them. They would work productively in our economy. But that is not a feasible political solution.

Two final points. One is on the specific circumstances like Angola. The first thing one has to decide is, How important is Angola to us? Do we care if there is a Marxist-Leninist regime in Angola? Why not let the South Africans take care of it, as they are perfectly capable of doing? Why do we have to worry about Angola?

Second, we could say that it is indeed a problem for us, but it is a problem that will resolve itself. All those Cuban troops will come down with AIDS; they'll all eventually be withdrawn, and we won't have to take any decisive action in the case of Angola.

Or we can say now that Angola is absolutely crucial. I'm not in a position to make this decision. I'm not an expert even on the geography of Africa. But if we say that Angola is crucial to the United States, we cannot permit a so-called Marxist-Leninist regime to survive there. We must take action. We would not invade Angola; we would just tell Cuba to get its troops out. What the hell are 30,000 or 40,000 Cuban troops doing in Angola? If we say they shouldn't be there, we should tell Cuba that they shouldn't be there and that we will not let them be there, even if that means stopping Cuban ships on the high seas.

Similar decisions must be made on Mozambique and Cambodia. Whatever decision we make on Angola has nothing to do with democracy in Angola. There will not be any democracy in Angola or in Mozambique or in Cambodia. But it does have to do with the strategic relations between the Soviet Union and the United States. As for lying in Washington, I'm a newcomer to Washington. In New York, of course, no one lies.

I don't mind witnesses before congressional committees being put under oath. I think congressmen should be put under oath at the same time. And since congressmen lie to the American people all the time, I find it a little hard to take their sanctimonious statements about lying to the American people all that seriously.

Sometimes rulers and governors do have to lie to the people. The notion that the American government should never lie to the American people is nonsense. Of course, it should lie to the American people only in those circumstances where lying is necessary for reasons of national security. That has always been the case. Every American administration has lied to the people. Every government in the world, ever, has lied to its people, when circumstances made it necessary. So I just don't take this business of lying seriously. It's a lot of congressional sanctimoniousness.

Mr. DeMuth: I would like to turn to the audience for questions.

Question: I'd like to hear the panelists address the question of how to build and sustain the support of the American people for a Reagan Doctrine or something like it—I know you're uncomfortable with the idea of a doctrine. You've all agreed that there are points where this kind of intervention is necessary, and yet, in order to be successful, there has to be a network of support groups among the American people that will sustain it.

The other side has recognized that very well. As you know, they've built quite an impressive network of support for the anti-intervention movement through CISPES—the Committee in Solidarity with the People of El Salvador—and other organizations. They have had a big impact on Congress. They have mobilized and targeted districts, perhaps even Mr. Solarz's district, to create the impression that large numbers of people oppose our actions in Angola, Nicaragua, and other places.

To carry out the other policy, there has to be some way of building a similar kind of network and support mechanism among the American people. And in order to do that, don't we need more than just a case-by-case approach? Don't we need some kind of over-arching doctrine or some appealing framework with which to galvanize American public support?

Mr. Kristol: A government gets support—and this is certainly true of the United States—for its foreign ventures, not by talking to the people but by doing things, by mobilizing the people behind action, not behind words. The doing has to be articulated in a sensible and rational way, but I know of no case in American history when the president or the Congress decided that power had to be projected and failed to receive the support of the American people, at least initially. If the American people had been asked whether they should go into World War I, I'm not sure what the vote would have been. I know what the vote would have been on World War II prior to the attack on Pearl Harbor. And if Germany had not declared war on the United States, we probably would never have gone to war with Hitler's Germany, there was so little sentiment for it.

Opinion in foreign policy is mobilized by doing things, not by taking polls. If the action has been thought through, if it makes sense, and if why it makes sense can be explained, and if then it can be done with a reasonable chance of success, the people will support it.

MR. HARRIES: I agree that a successful action is probably the best way of selling this. But there is always a declaratory and an operational aspect to foreign policy, and the question of keeping them in proper relationship to each other is an important one. The strongest claim that one can make for the Reagan Doctrine is in this declaratory sense. It is good for simplifying a policy and making it understandable to the public—for mobilizing and motivating, for making comprehensible what seems messy otherwise.

There is a case for doctrine, but care has to be taken in becoming inspirational for declaratory purposes. There are real dangers even in terms of getting the public support that is needed.

It is easy to pitch rhetoric to win short-term benefits, but the inevitable long-term outcome of overselling, especially when the opposition is alert, attentive, and well organized, will be cynicism and disillusionment. There is a problem with selling the Reagan Doctrine too hard, overblowing it, and making it carry a weight it is simply not constructed to sustain.

That is not an answer to your question. This is the wrong panel if you want to talk about how to set up networks and that sort of thing. I'm the wrong guy for that.

MR. ROSENFELD: The notion that CISPES and groups like it have overwhelmed American public opinion, the U.S. government, and the people who feel the other way is so remote from my understanding of the situation that I can't imagine what you're talking about.

MR. MURAVCHIK: I can imagine what you're talking about, but I'm with Owen Harries in not answering your question about setting up networks. But I'm not with Owen in worrying about overly inspiring the American people. One of the liabilities we have had started with a decision by President Johnson to avoid overinspiring the American people about the stakes of the Vietnam conflict. That was an important early error, it seems to me. A similar error was made early by the Reagan administration, which did not announce a Reagan Doctrine until Charles Krauthammer pointed out that it was in effect what they were doing.

It may have been a perfect example of what Irving Kristol recommends, which is taking action without articulating it. It is a perfect example of how in various situations that can be enormously ineffective. One of the keys to the problem the Reagan administration has had in sustaining support for its policies is that it didn't start out clearly. The administration is still loath to articulate the global issues involved and to invest the president's political capital in his policies in a way that would indicate to the people that the stakes for the country are indeed very high. The key to what makes it possible to rally public opinion—if we would do it—is that the kinds of policies we're talking about have a crucial dual virtue—they are right and serve our ideals, and they are necessary and serve our self-interest.

QUESTION: I agree with Mr. Kristol that action is very important. A perceptive columnist wrote a few years ago that Nicaragua is not Vietnam; it's eight times smaller in population and area and eight times closer to us. His name was Stephen Rosenfeld.

We can see that the Reagan Doctrine is nothing but the Monroe Doctrine when it is applied to the Western Hemisphere and force is used. Our great presidents have invoked it—Teddy Roosevelt, Woodrow Wilson. Even Lyndon Johnson put Marines into the Dominican Republic about twenty years ago.

Abraham Lincoln threatened to use force to throw the French out of Mexico. Today's Congress would have impeached him. Lincoln plainly said that if the French did not stop supporting Maximilian, he would march the troops down when the Civil War ended. They stopped. The Mexicans threw him out. The point is, force can be successful.

The president of Chad pointed out that our bombing of Libya was a tremendous political success. It shocked Qaddafi and contributed to the morale that allowed Chad to sweep the Libyans from the northern part of the country. The action in Grenada was a tremendous political success.

Can we not do this in Nicaragua? Of course we can. It simply requires the same courage that Lincoln had, that Teddy Roosevelt, Woodrow Wilson, and Truman had. I think even John Kennedy would have acted. The only thing wrong with Professor Kristol's point about invasion is television. The American public cannot sustain a long war when the television reporters show American casualties and things we did wrong but do not show the opposition.

But there is a simple answer, and the answer comes from Congressman Solarz. In a foreign policy report, he said the key is to analyze the difference between national security interests and political interests. Much as I want democracy in Managua, I don't think the Marines marching in is the solution. But our national security interests are absolutely clear. I could go on in detail, having been in the intelligence community, about their slow, steady, careful buildup. In ten or fifteen years, Nicaragua will be like Cuba. We could conduct a simple three- or four-day air and naval action with not a single American soldier touching the soil of Nicaragua, simply attacking Soviet installations, their helicopters, and their 10,000-foot airfield designed for Soviet bombers and reconnaissance. We have already warned that we would act if Migs were delivered, but it was a mistake to allow MI-24 helicopters, which are being used effectively to slaughter Afghan guerrillas. The Soviet general staff is enjoying testing MI-24s in tropical jungle territory against poor, brown-skinned peasants. Morally, we should not think that is a good thing.

If we deprived Nicaragua of modern Soviet technology, the killing would go on but at a much lower level, with rifles and machine guns rather than with tanks and helicopters. The moral impact on Ortega would be like that on Qaddafi. It might be such a tremendous shock that the contras, the freedom fighters, could take control in a few years. I think this is practical, and it can be done.

And the last point, Mr. Harries, you don't take leadership by the latest poll. Franklin Roosevelt took leadership in helping the British in World War II when, as Mr. Kristol says, we were overwhelmingly isolationist. You take leadership, as Abraham Lincoln did and as Teddy Roosevelt, Woodrow Wilson, Franklin Roosevelt, and Harry Truman did.

MR. KRISTOL: Can I say something about television? I like your remarks—they're very sensible. But there is a misapprehension as to what television or battle scenes would do to the American people. I'm not worried about television making pacifists of the American people. I am rather worried about its brutalizing the American people. That's the more likely effect of television on the American sentiment and on American morale.

I don't think seeing war on television makes people antiwar, any more than seeing war in the movies makes people antiwar, or seeing action dramas on television makes people antishooting. A brilliant essay was written in the 1930s by a pro-Communist literary critic, Kenneth Burke, who argued persuasively that all the antiwar movies and all the antiwar novels had the perverse and ironic effect of making people more understanding of war and more accepting of war. So I'm not worried about television. I mean, there's a myth that everyone would say, "Oh my goodness, people are getting killed." I think we might become too bloodthirsty. I don't think we might become too pacifist.

QUESTION: If the panel would indulge me, I've been trying to set down what the differences that separate you are, and I've been trying to come to grips with Josh Muravchik's central question, which is, If we do not have a quest for democracy as our banner—and I take "banner" to be the operative word—what is the alternative? I've tried to write down what the choices are, and I'd like to get some clarification from Josh on his position on a question that I would pose to you.

I take it that the first choice is that we simply acquiesce in Soviet interventionism on behalf of insurgent movements that they justify as being in support of national liberation against colonialist or racist regimes. I would assume that all the members of the panel would agree that is unacceptable. We cannot simply acquiesce.

The second choice, it seems to me, is something Irving Kristol has suggested, that we have a policy of counterintervention. This is the anti-Brezhnev doctrine that acts as a check. That still doesn't deal with the issue of a banner, because if all we do is say that when you intervene we will intervene, it wouldn't satisfy Josh. That's not a positive banner.

It seems to me that we do have a positive banner, even though it may sound cornballish perhaps to Irving Kristol—the banner of the UN Charter. The banner of the UN Charter has essentially been nonintervention. That is, we and the Soviet Union have to agree that we cannot intervene, whether it's on behalf of democracy or on behalf of freedom from colonialists or a racist group.

I myself would support the concept of the Reagan Doctrine within that context. That is to say, the Reagan Doctrine is not our end. Our banner is not democracy; our banner is nonintervention. But since we cannot get the Soviet Union to behave that way, we reserve for ourselves—and those are the key words—we reserve for ourselves the right to act accordingly. Then we don't have to get into any questions about doctrine, about boxing ourselves in, because we can

44

do whatever we wish. We simply reserve to ourselves the right to act differently.

But I take it that your point, Josh, is that you would go beyond having the Reagan Doctrine simply be counterinterventionist. Or am I mistaken in believing that it is your position that even if we could reach an accord with the Soviets to comply with the UN Charter on nonintervention and respect for the sovereign equality of all states, you would say no, it should be our doctrine to roll back communism, to roll back those advances the Communists have made?

MR. MURAVCHIK: That's a good question, but my answer is this: If we could achieve an agreement with the Soviet Union that we had any reason to believe was enforceable, would be complied with, and would make them begin to live by the letter of the UN Charter, that would be an offer we couldn't refuse. It would be a wonderful new day, indeed, but it would still leave the question of the well-being of the peoples who suffer under Communist rule as well as other forms of tyranny.

And my response would then be that I would favor continuing to wage political struggle to encourage them to throw off that yoke and free themselves. That is not forbidden to us under the terms of the UN Charter. In fact a good case can be made that if the benchmark here is mutual adherence to the terms of the UN Charter, the Communist regimes would have to begin dismantling themselves. In terms of the charter provisions spelled out in the Universal Declaration of Human Rights, those governments violate the UN Charter. The existence of those governments may not be per se a violation of the UN Charter, but the things that they do every moment of every day are violations. If the governments would not have to dismantle themselves, they would radically have to transform their method of relating to their own citizenry.

But since I am very doubtful, and I suspect you are too, that the Soviet Union would join us in a regime of obedience to the UN Charter, then for us to make that our banner seems to me to be a feckless policy indeed. The much more effective banner for us is the preamble to the U.S. Declaration of Independence. We should simply assert that we endorse the fulfillment of rights by individuals everywhere. We have lots of evidence that individuals everywhere are yearning for the fulfillment of those rights and welcome our endorsement or whatever support we can lend them.

MR. KRISTOL: I just want to go on record as saying that I thoroughly deplore in this serious conversation on foreign policy, any mention of the UN Charter.

MR. DEMUTH: With that, I'd like to thank all of our panelists, and thank all of you for the rapt attention that the panelists have enjoyed.